MOTHER GOOSE and GRIMM'S
NIGHT OF THE LIVING VACUUM!

by Mike Peters

TOPPER BOOKS

AN IMPRINT OF PHAROS BOOKS • A SCRIPPS HOWARD COMPANY

NEW YORK

Library of Congress Cataloging-in-Publication Data
Peters, Mike, 1943–
    (Mother Goose & Grimm. Selections)
    Mother Goose & Grimm's night of the living vacuum /
by Mike Peters.
        p.   cm.
    ISBN 0-88687-519-6 : $8.95
    I. Title.   II. Title: Mother Goose and Grimm's night
of the living vacuum.
PN6728.M67P47   1991
741.5'973—dc20   91-16493   CIP

Printed in the United States of America

Topper Books
An Imprint of Pharos Books
A Scripps Howard Company
200 Park Avenue
New York, NY 10166

Pharos Books are available at special discounts on bulk
purchases for sales promotions, premiums, fundraising
or educational use. For details contact the Special Sales
Department, Pharos Books, 200 Park Avenue, New York,
NY 10166. (212) 692-3766.

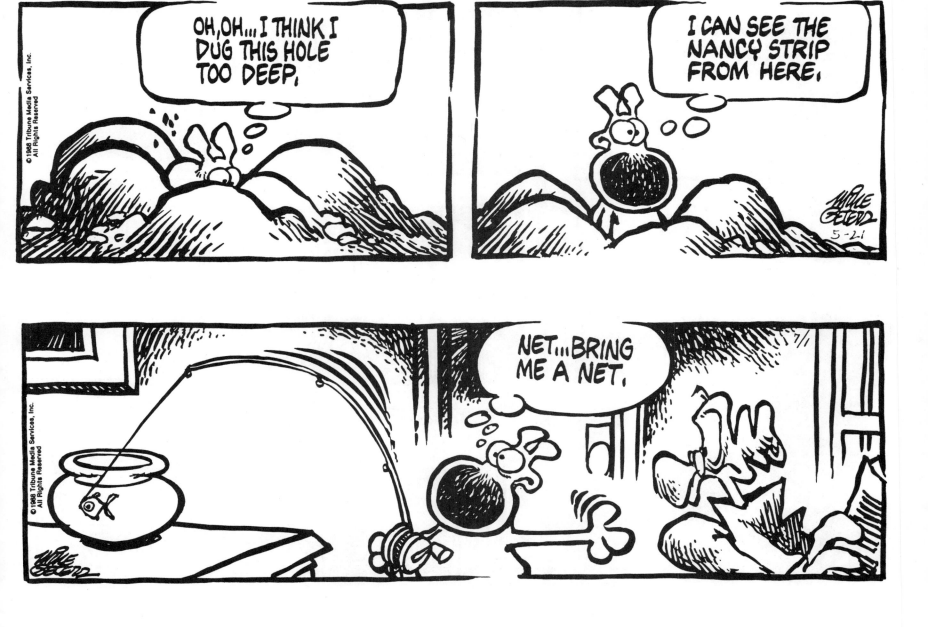

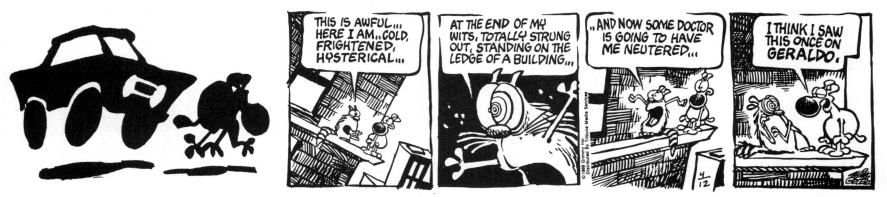

GENERAL PATTON

COLONEL NORTH

MAJOR WEDGEY

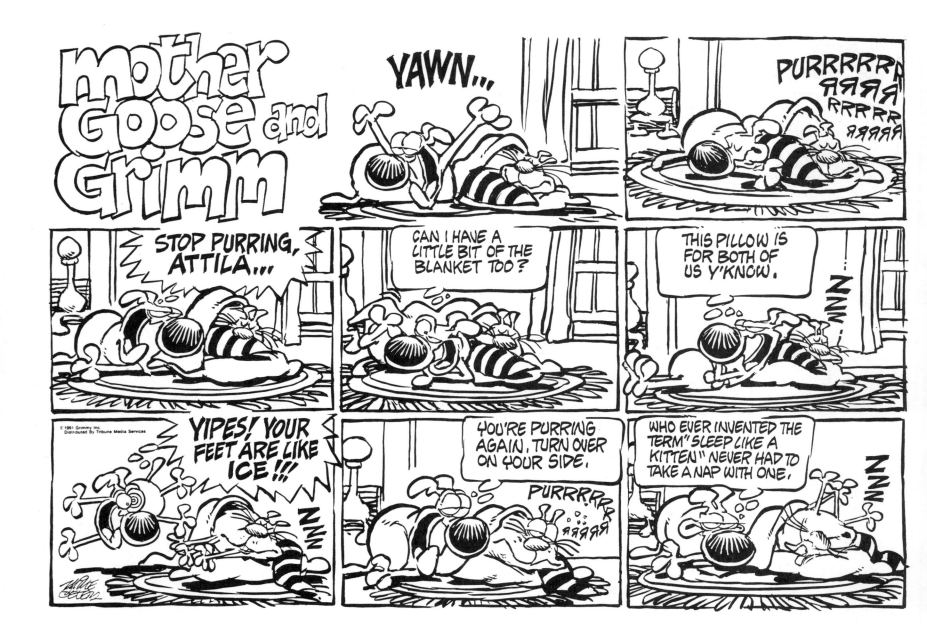

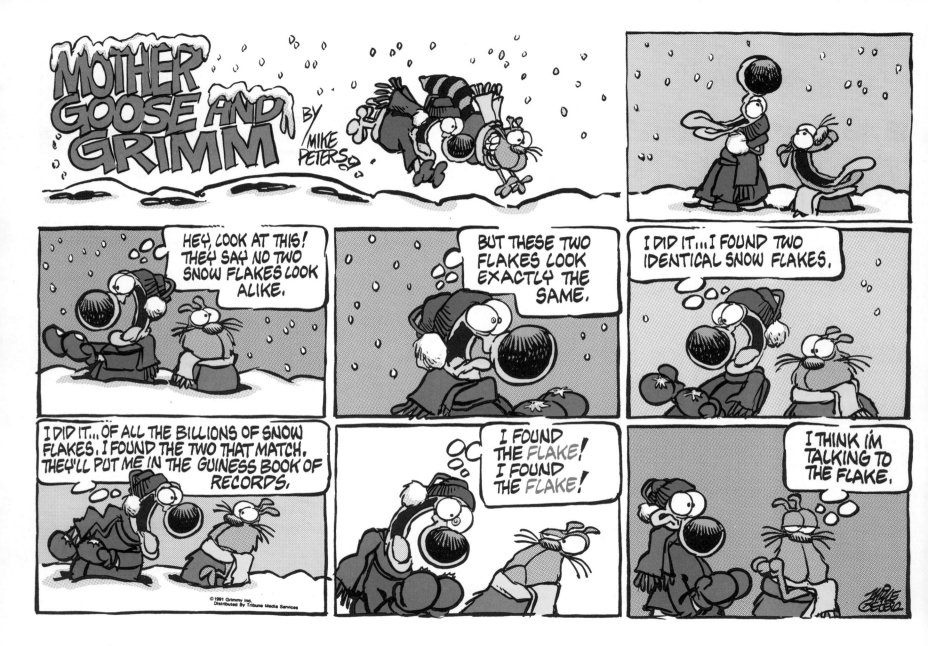

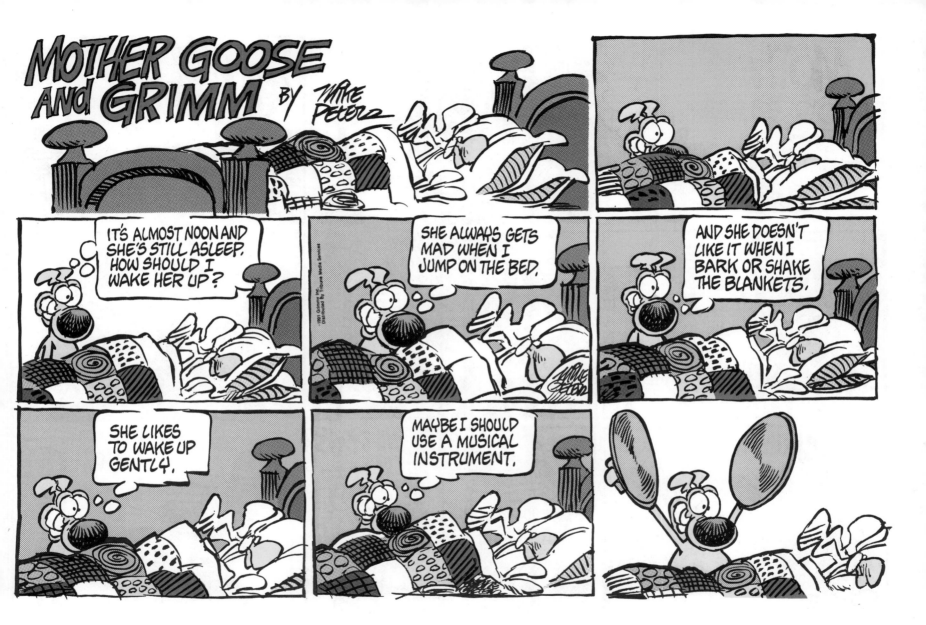

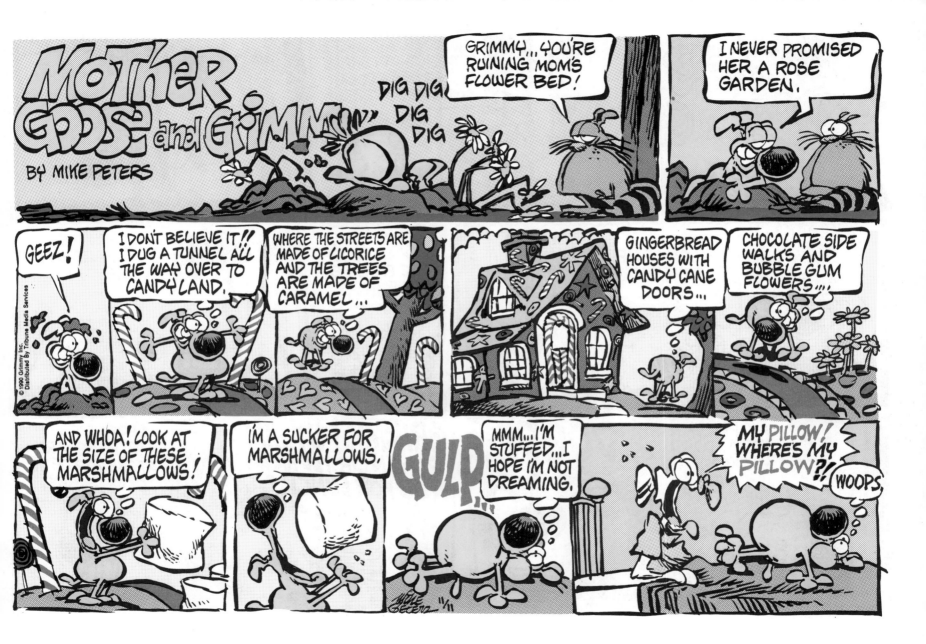

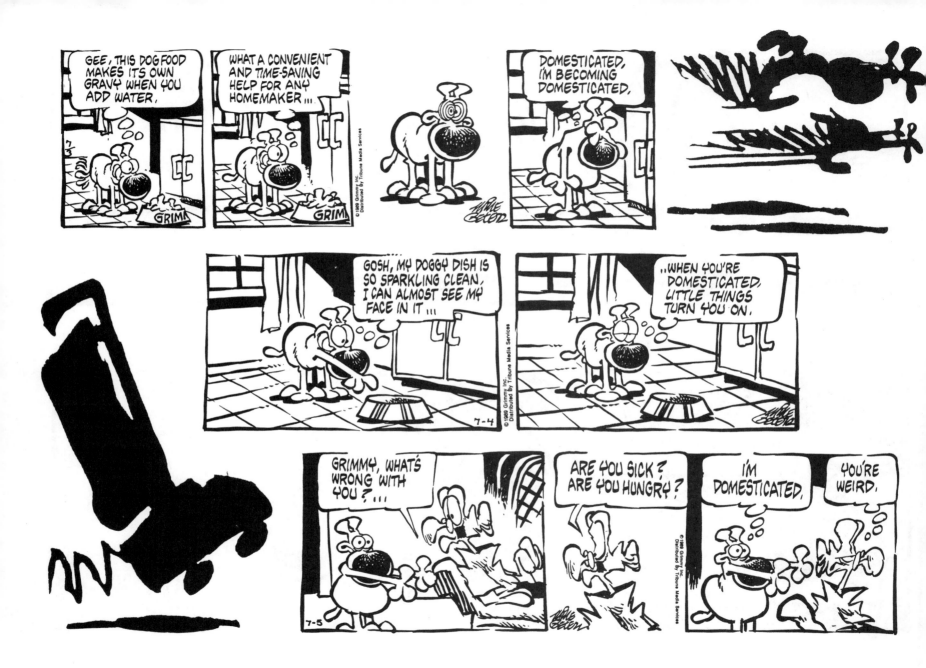

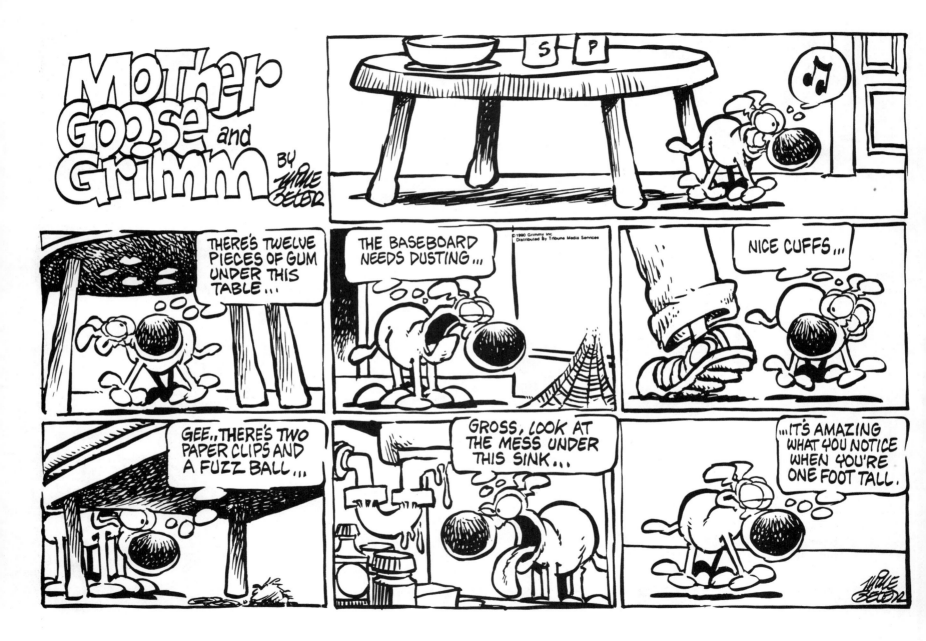

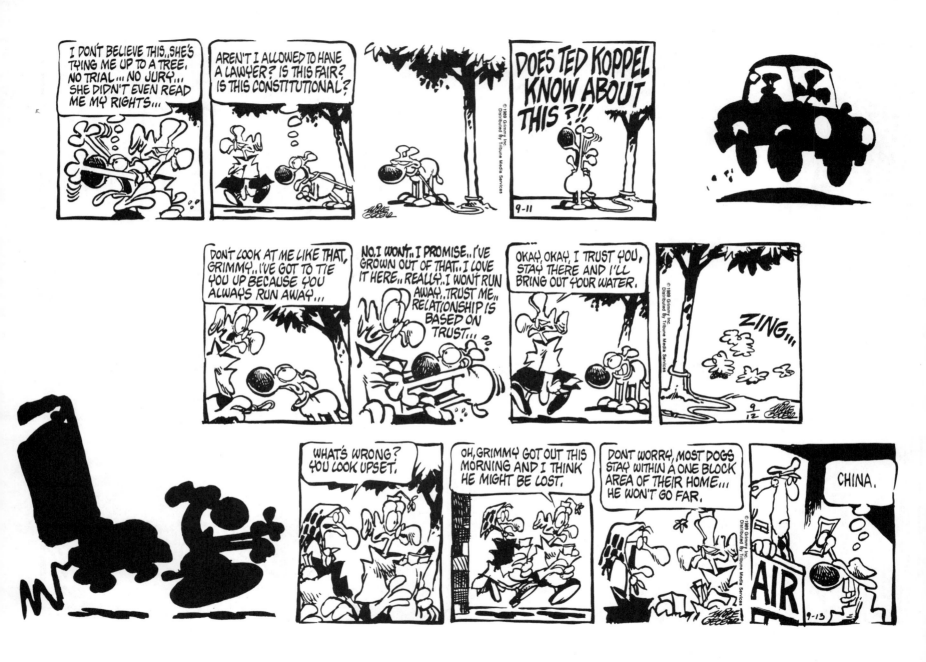

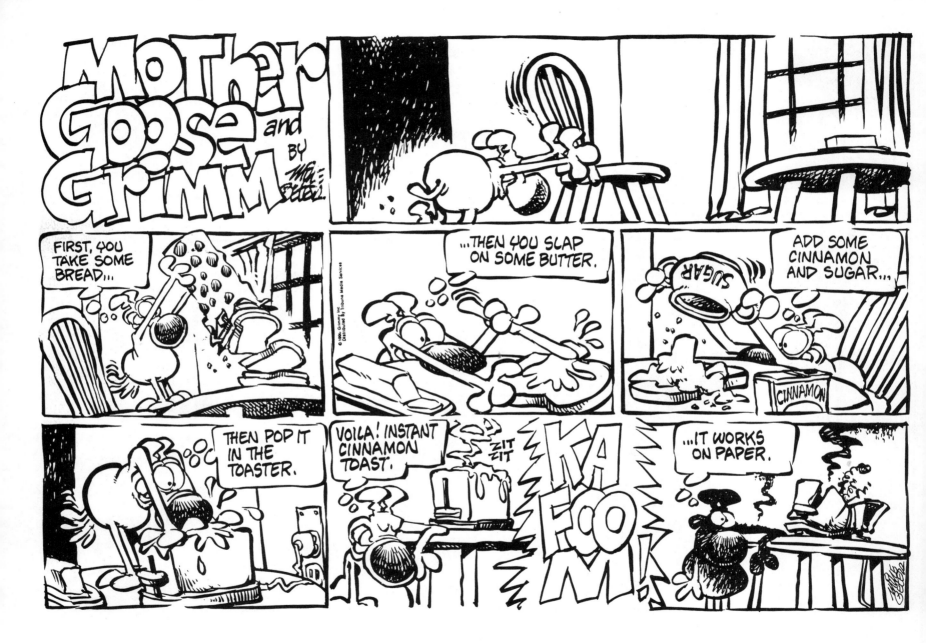

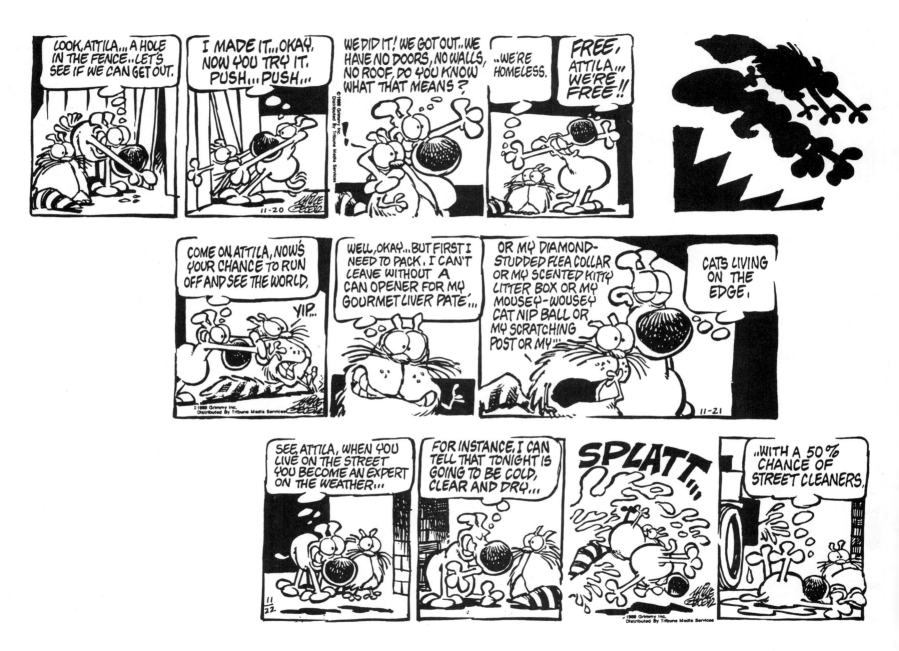

9-21

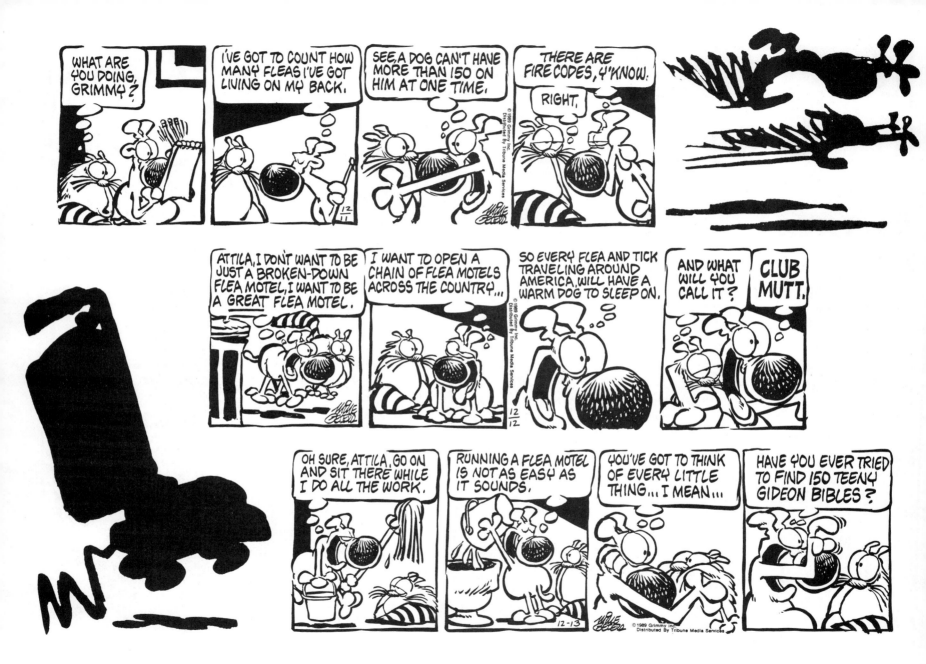

12-14

© 1989 Grimmy Inc.
Distributed By Tribune Media Services

© 1989 Grimmy Inc.
Distributed By Tribune Media Services

12-15

© 1989 Grimmy Inc.
Distributed By Tribune Media Services

12-16

Heeeeeeeeeeeeeeeeere's
GRIMMY
TM

Now you can order all four MOTHER GOOSE & GRIMM books!

✂ ---

Please send me

_____ copies of STEEL-BELTED GRIMM at **$5.95** each

_____ copies of 4-WHEEL GRIMMY at **$6.95** each

_____ copies of GRIMMY COME HOME at **$6.95** each

_____ copies of NIGHT OF THE LIVING VACUUM at **$8.95** each

_____ TOTAL BOOKS (Please add .50 per book for postage and handling)

My check for $ _____ is enclosed.

Ship to

NAME _____

ADDRESS _____

CITY _____ STATE _____ ZIP _____

Make check payable to PHAROS BOOKS. Send order to: Sales Dept., Pharos Books, 200 Park Ave., NYC, NY 10166. Please allow 4-6 weeks for delivery.